ANGRY LEADERSHIP

My Seven Guiding Principles of Leadership

ANGRY LEADERSHIP

My Seven Guiding Principles of Leadership

VICTOR ANGRY

Freeze Time Media

ISBN-13: 978-1-946702-10-4

ISBN-10: 1-946702-10-2

Front Cover Photo Courtesy Minnesota National Guard Public Affairs Office, by Tech. Sgt. Lynette Hoke

This book is dedicated in loving memory of Ma: my mother, Joanne Lomax-Angry. She sacrificed her personal time to give her seven children a lifetime.

NEVER PERSONAL
ALWAYS PROFESSIONAL!

[illegible] 23 JAN 19

Acknowledgments

"A miracle-worker is an artist of the soul. There is no higher art than living a good life."

Marianne Williamson

I WANT TO believe that I've helped paint many souls, and my hope is that each of those souls are living a good life because of it. I have had many artists at work with my soul, and my life is good because of them. I want to thank the following for all their miracle work:

My father David Angry for marrying my mother and bringing seven beautiful little Angry souls into this world. I'll never truly understand why you walked out; what I do understand is why you walked in.

Joanne Lomax-Angry, for sacrificing your dreams and your life to raise seven children on your own. You are my first artist, my miracle worker. and I love you and thank you to the depths of my soul.

Ms. Brenda Patterson, what more can I say but thank you, thank you, thank you! You saw more in me, which helped me see more in myself.

Each of my siblings: Timothy, Reginald, Regina, Carol, Victoria, and David II for always loving me when it got hard for me to love myself. We, ARE family!

Emil F. Meiz III, a name I will never forget because of the compassion you showed a young, distraught private after I found out my young cousin had died. You were the first military leader I modeled myself after.

My CAASO family, there are too many of you to name, but I'm sure you all will agree that my two lead miracle workers were Gladys Cason and John Tilley. All of you played a role in developing my soul, but they rolled the plays at a time in my young career where I was at the crossroads of a good life and the road to nowhere.

Miriam Wallace, Jerry Seimer, Joey Starr, my JOSAC plank holders, OSAC/ OSAA and family.

Art Sosa, receiving your personal phone call at my mother's home on the morning of her funeral, sharing your condolences, was so off guard, yet needed, that it is a vision forever etched in my mind, a definite core memory, and I thank you for that, sir.

Fred Chesbro, car salesmen are there to sell me cars, sir.

Timothy McCoy, my guardian angel who was in the right place at the right time and more than likely, saved my life. I know it, you know it, and God appreciates it.

My dear friend Setu Taifane, you were the epitome of passion and a true leader of virtue. I miss you my friend. Thank you for all the many talks.

Matt Jordan: Batman, we ran a great command as first sergeant and company commander — that's what dynamic duos do.

My brothers and sisters from USASMA Class 55, aka Double Nickel.

My National Guard Bureau Office of Equal Opportunity and Civil Rights family.

Felton Page, my wise ranger and mentor. Thank you for all your council and very embellished stories (you gotta be in the family to know it, right?) I really miss the Monday morning roundtable discussions.

My OSACOM family led by Mike Bishop. Sir, thank you for the opportunity to serve as your command sergeant major and being the other half of your command team. I've seen you work a lot of miracles and never stand in the way of soldier progression. I never had the opportunity to thank you for your faith and confidence in me as we figured out what the final plan would be with me holding down two seats, that as the OSACOM CSM and the CSM of the Army National Guard. It all worked itself out in the end.

And last but certainly not least, Major General Raymond Carpenter. I remember sitting in the green room just before we walked into a standing room only for my retirement ceremony and asking you, "Why me?" Your response is ingrained in my brain forever: "You were the right person for the job." My hope is that we painted some souls that are still proudly displayed today and that you are living a really good life.

Contents

Foreword

ANGRY LEADERSHIP IS a must read for anyone who has an interest in leadership. Whether you are young and aspiring to be a great leader, a professional who is seeking career advancement, or someone who has personal leadership skills that need improvement, this straightforward "how to" style manual will provide the necessary coaching from basic to more advanced leadership.

As the acting director of the Army National Guard in 2009, I was faced with selecting an interim command sergeant major to replace CSM John Gipe, who had accepted another position. As I surveyed the potential candidates, CSM Victor Angry came immediately to mind. I was impressed from our first meeting. He embodied all of the traits of a picture perfect command sergeant major, he conducted himself as a professional, he was a striking figure in uniform, he was the model of physical fitness, he had a terrific relationship with soldiers, and he was an exceptional leader who most importantly lead by example!

I knew whoever filled the position was faced with overcoming the added burden of being an interim CSM whose term in the job was dependent upon the timing of the process to appoint the next permanent CSM. I was confident the interim status would not be an obstacle for CSM Angry and he would perform at the highest level!

He willingly accepted the challenge of being "the interim" Army National Guard command sergeant major, and we quickly became an effective leadership team for the benefit of the entire Army National Guard. To this day, I am impressed with CSM Angry and have no doubt I made the right decision when I selected him for the top enlisted job in the Army National Guard!

This book outlines CSM Angry's life journey and the leadership lessons learned at each turn. He provides real life examples of his experience in developing his seven principles of leadership. The vignettes are engaging, entertaining, and are situations to which we all can relate. CSM Angry provides a "how to" clear, concise guide on doing the right thing to ensure you are "lucky" when the timing is right. I believe this book will soon find its way onto the reading lists of experienced leaders!

Major General (Ret.) Ray Carpenter

Obsession

I WAS BORN to lead. I finally realized this at the age of forty-three when I was sitting in my home office three months after my retirement from the United States Army National Guard. I recall the conversation I had with my older brother, Reg, more than twenty years ago. He told me that I would be miserable working in the private sector because, as he put it, "You like helping people." After serving my country for over twenty-three years, I have found that to lead is to serve, and I continue doing that today by serving my community as a volunteer firefighter.

I had a very successful military career that heavily influenced the person I am today. I entered the Army as an enlisted soldier and rose through the ranks from a private (E-1) to the highest enlisted rank of sergeant major (E-9). I cultivated my career as the first African American to hold the position as command sergeant major of the Army National Guard. If I were asked what two things helped propel me to the top of my career, I would honestly have to say they were "luck" and "timing." Let me explain, because as basic as they sound, I did a lot of prep work throughout my career to be on the *lucky list* and put myself in the best position for the universe to provide the most perfect timing. In other words, if you're going to be *the one*, someone has to see *the one*.

I first heard the words luck and timing when I was assigned to the Comprehensive Review Working Group (CRWG) for Don't Ask, Don't Tell in 2010. It was in a conversation I had with now retired Lieutenant General Gregory Biscone. We were conversing about our military careers and I asked him how, out of all the thousands of Air Force aviators, he was one of the few selected to fly the B-2 Stealth Bomber. His response was, "A lot of that was luck and timing." I responded quickly with, "Tell me about it; I know that very well!"

That's when he explained to me his definition of luck and timing. He said that luck and timing is a very short list of well-prepared leaders who have done everything asked of them, and then some, and who have made themselves invisibly visible (meaning opportunity sees you; you don't see opportunity — your service is truly selfless). He went on to tell me that when opportunities do arise, leaders go to the list, and you'll never know you're on it until you're called. That made perfect sense to me, because I've always just loved to serve and take care of others. My motto to my soldiers was always, "Don't chase the rank; let the rank chase you! If it catches you, then you know you were meant to wear it." This principle applies to the progression process in general.

As I look back on my career, I want to share with you these seven disciplines of leadership that helped me attain a milestone in my life that I am honored and humbled to have achieved. As I reflect on my career, I realize that I could not have done any of it without any one of these seven guiding principles.

I've broken down these principles by chapter:

(Foundation) My purpose: Every solid tree must have a strong root.

(Reinforced Words) Information overload: Negative words are a root cause of suicides; positive words created my greatness!

(Mentors) My A-Team: If you aren't adding a mentor a month, you're missing the point!

(Fitness) The Total Package: A strong body complements a strong mind.

(Tenacity) Keep a full plate: I do more before 7 a.m. than most people do all day.

(Preparation) Add yourself to the List: You have no control over luck and timing, but you can be prepared.

(Self-evaluation) How am I doing? Self-evaluation is important. Group evaluation is a must! Both evaluations answered one question for me: Did I buy in?

(The Crossroad) The Collision of Luck and Timing) Where my preparation met the perfect opportunity.

1

Foundation

"Your name right now is synonymous with success."

Sgt. Maj. (Ret.) Anson Smith

ONE OF THE most important things I figured out in my life was that before I could lead anyone, I had to take charge of and lead myself. That was the hardest of my seven disciplines to accomplish, and it remains a work in progress to this day. I couldn't have come to the realization that I was good at leading on my own, mainly because I wasn't leading myself — hell, I didn't even believe in myself.

How I did it wasn't a formula or a mission statement I developed sitting in the barrack. What I can say about my process was that I was a very fortunate young man that had many blessings raining down on me, many angels waiting in the mist to guide me, and two ladies named Grace and Mercy that deflected many bad decisions I made along the way. In other words, my journey to accomplishing and excelling at my climb to and through leadership was far from planned; it was in large a process of looking, listening, and learning, with lots of action on my part. It took me a long time before I would recognize what good leaders noticed in me and why they invested so much extra time in developing me.

The whole concept of an Army career is progression and leadership development, so it's not unusual for any leader to guide you to what "right" looks like. It's those that invested that extra time who saw in me what I had been feeling all my life — that I can be a great leader. Luckily, I was disciplined enough to listen and do what they told me back in those days. I would eventually sharpen my skills and widen my radar to search for good leadership and develop my own skills, recognizing those skillsets that felt comfortable for me in my decision-making and leadership styles. This is when I started seeing my purpose in life really develop. This book isn't about verifying textbook definitions or an attempt to rewrite them. It's solely about how I was able to successfully navigate my life through the military and achieve the highest honor of an enlisted soldier, that of having the title of command sergeant major of the Army National Guard.

A part of the definition of leadership states that for it to work, one must provide an individual with purpose, direction, and motivation. Purpose for me was and is a necessity not only for building successful teams, but also for building my life. Once I realized and admitted to myself that I absolutely and genuinely loved helping soldiers and helping others, it became my purpose, and that set my base foundation that I would stand on. Once I got both of my feet on solid ground, I stood tall, knowing that what I was standing on was anchored and unmovable. Now I just needed to answer the question: What am I standing for?

After all, everyone knows that a man who stands for nothing will fall for anything. I stood for Truth, Justice, and the American way! Come on now, you had to see that one coming (lol). On more than one occasion I have made a decision that I felt right about but changed it to go with the majority, so I wouldn't be ostracized. It only took a few times of me doing this and hating myself for not standing by my decision before I made a conscious change to always stand by my decision, no matter the outcome, and that I would always stand for righteousness. That is doing the right thing for the right reasons all the time. What I can tell you about this is that the decisions you make today are the difference in the solid structure you're building on for tomorrow. I've learned that if you follow up a bad decision with another bad decision, eventually you notice that the entire structure is built of cards, and a house built of cards will eventually fall.

One thing I can say about standing on your morals is that even when you feel deep in your heart that what you are doing is right, it will always be wrong to someone, somewhere. This brought great clarification to me of the saying, "You can please some of the people some of the time, but you can't please all of the people all of the time." Understanding that the personnel are the most important asset, I would make it a strong point to base my decisions on what's best for the organization. That sounds simple now, but it was a delicate balancing act then. This is where being color blind worked in my favor, because while most things are black and white to me, I also saw the gray areas and used that to my advantage.

Army enlisted leadership generally starts at the E-5 sergeant level, with a few exceptions. I was fortunate when I was promoted to the rank of sergeant because my promotion orders arrived a month before I was scheduled for a Permanent Change of Station (PCS) to Korea. This was fortunate for me because one of the hardest transitions to make in ranks is that from a specialist to a sergeant. The transition was harder if the soldier was promoted in the same command, or even worse, the same company.

Keeping it very basic, the Army has two positions, the leader and the led. Putting grades to titles, the leader within the enlisted ranks starts from the pay grade of E-5 through E-9 and the led is E-1 through E-4. Simply put, when an individual achieves the rank of E-5, he is charged with the authority/responsibility to correct violations of the Uniform Code of Military Justice (UCMJ). That authority reigns in both direction over junior service member to the most senior. The only thing that separates a junior NCO from a senior NCO is their levels of responsibility. The higher you go in rank, the more you are responsible for. In my days, junior soldiers were a very tight-knit group; it was a sad day to watch one of your fellow specialists get promoted to sergeant. It was a feeling as if they were lost to the dark side and gone forever — that is until you are promoted and join them.

To us it was like losing a "lost boy" to adulthood; we knew they would never see Neverland again. Or losing that last baby tooth and there goes the tooth fairy! There was no grace period to "test drive" your new rank and get accustomed to now being a leader. It was expected of you to no longer run with the pack, but to lead it. That generally got you a lot of enemies, because there's always a few who don't understand the transition you've just made and expect you to bend rules and break laws for them. However, I was spared this challenging process by only having to be in the command for a few weeks as a sergeant and spending that time to out-process the unit. By the time I arrived at my next assignment in Korea, I wore sergeant stripes on my uniform. As far as anyone knew (outside of the commander and the admin office), that's who I'd always been. That meant that none of the lower enlisted (E-1 through E-4), nor most of my peers and senior leaders, had expectations of me being anything other than a junior leader, which made my transition to leading less challenging.

This is where what I was standing on and what I was standing for would be tested. After being in the replacement battalion in Yongsan District of Korea for a few days, I was finally assigned to the 4th Battalion of the 501st Aviation Regiment at Camp Page. This was truly a training battalion as life stationed in Korea consisted of eating, sleeping and training, and we were excellent at it. On one training mission, after being at it for twelve hours, I fell asleep in the cab of our deuce and a half truck, which was configured as our communications RAT Rig, as we called it. I was awakened by a conversation between two senior noncommissioned. They were discussing a plan to have a junior soldier put out of the Army because they didn't like his attitude, which many times frustrated them. Their issue with this soldier was that he was too smart — smarter than both of them combined — and his level of intelligence was intimidating to them, which was not an acceptable quality to have in the 1980s Army.

When I'd heard enough, I stepped out of the truck, making a point to slam the door, so they could hear me. They both turned in my direction, looking directly at me, and quickly walked away.

What I'd observed about this soldier wasn't that he was a smart ass in response to them or thought he was better than them; he had what I would now call the Einstein effect. He didn't have the ability to "dumb it down" to their conversation levels. He would always offer a better solution to their directives without thinking that in the 1980s Army leadership, with him being the led, it was easier to do as you're told and get it done in the most efficient way possible rather than challenging or questioning authority.

I found this soldier to be a true blessing to the command. He had 20th century concepts in the 19th century! Prior to overhearing their conversation, this soldier became one of my go-to soldiers in the command. I've always been good with identifying personalities, and this soldier had a good one. He was so damn smart that when you gave him a task with directions, he really had some outstanding alternative ways of getting them done. Unfortunately, in the late 1980s, thinking outside the box wasn't only not heard of, but it was also a definite no-go at any station. Once I sat him down and discussed my role as the leader and his role as the led, and that there was a time and a place where he could be creative with tasks assigned to him and other times where it had to be done to my standard, we operated as a team should operate. I'd give him a task to complete using his own processes, and then I'd give him specific tasks to complete with specific directions. I noticed he stopped questioning and began to enjoy the command and the leader/ led process. I didn't know at that time that I was using some of the categories of leadership — the delegating and authoritative processes. I just knew that's what he needed to succeed, based on my conversation with him and what I observed from watching him.

The next day after this incident, I reported what I overheard to the company commander because the E-8 (who was the problem) was the acting first sergeant and if I didn't do something fast, this soldier would be unjustly removed from the Army. It was at that time that I knew I was loyal to the Army, and loyalty to the Army was the umbrella that outranks any level of loyalty under it.

What happened next is one of the reasons I'm happy that the Whistleblower Protection Act is in place today. I was called into the first sergeant's office to be read an Article 15 stating conduct unbecoming of a noncommissioned officer and that I violated the code of the noncommissioned officer. This man was coming after me because I stood up for the soldier; his interpretation of loyalty was that I should have stood up and supported the Corp, the Noncommissioned Officer Corp. While it's funny today, nineteen years ago I was terrified and thought, *How in the hell can I get an Article 15 for standing up for a soldier who was being wrongfully targeted?* I fought it with character letters from each of my soldiers and a few senior officers that knew my character even in the beginning. The higher it went, the more the truth came out, and I was eventually excused from the charge with no further retaliation.

That was my first foundational stance that confirmed to me what I stood on and what I stood for. That one single stance earned me complete respect from my subordinates and many of my peers and confirmed to me what

I knew I would be doing for the next twenty years: taking care of soldiers.

2

Reinforced Words

"I see more in you than you see in yourself."

Brenda Patterson

"STICKS AND STONES may break my bones, but words will never hurt me." Well that wasn't true. They hurt me a lot growing up; so much that my self-esteem was destroyed. I grew up with my two front teeth bigger than Baby New Year's ears. I would hear it from my siblings and the kids in school. One year the school Christmas play theme song was "All I want for Christmas is my two front teeth." The teachers decided I would be the prop. The class would sing, "All I want for Christmas is my two front teeth, my two front teeth, see my two front teeth." When they sang "see my two front teeth," I was the center of attention. I would smile to show my two front teeth, which were probably visible from Mars.

I even won the big teeth award (oddly enough, I seem to be the only person to ever have received that award). I really can't tell you what's worse, a tour of duty in Afghanistan or early childhood with big teeth. The truth is, I didn't know what self-esteem was. I was an eight-year-old black boy from the suburbs living a very basic life, not knowing anything about what life had planned for me. All I knew was that being picked on really sucked, and if crawling under a rock was actually an option, I'd more than likely still be there today. Thank God that self-esteem is a growing process, because I truly felt like a seed beneath the dirt, and with a little water and nurturing, I began to grow. I have several people to thank for their help, and I'll address a few of them in the Mentors chapter.

As I look back on my childhood, there were positive people with positive influences all around me. I just never noticed them or their positive words never penetrated like negativity did, but all that would change when I met Ms. Brenda Patterson. She was the one person who started me on my journey to manhood and ultimately becoming the command sergeant major of the Army National Guard.

Many people gave me a lot of knowledge throughout my military career; some of that knowledge was good stuff and some of it was terrible. I can sum this up with the best comment that was given to me by one of my aviators while I was stationed in Hawaii. It involved financial investing for the future and everyone had their own ideas of how I should best navigate this new adventure. Everything from which bank has the best returns, what to invest in, how long to invest, and how much to invest. After all of that, into my office walked Mr. Ross Steadman. He sat in the chair positioned right in front of my desk and said, "People are going to tell you a lot of things about investing. Take what you want from it, use it, and throw the rest away, but whatever you decide to do, do something now. As basic as that sounds, his comments were so profound that I was instantly drawn to listening to them and immediately took his advice. His comments taught me that all advice really IS good advice, and that some of that advice is absolutely transcending!

I enlisted in the Army at the age of seventeen under the Delayed Entry Program, which meant I was federal property during my last year of high school. That's not a normal thing for a seventeen-year-old black kid from a small town in Florida to do. There were those in my neighborhood who didn't think it was a smart decision. At forty-nine years old, looking back on my life I can tell you that was one of the smartest decisions I could have ever made. My decision to join was heavily influenced by ten words someone said to me during a time when my mother had given me permission to move out of the house and live with my Uncle Clifford; his girlfriend, Ms. Brenda; and his son, my first cousin, Terry. Terry was my right or left arm, depending on which side of the street we were walking on. We were inseparable and did almost everything together. We spent our childhood days bouncing between both of our mothers' homes where we grew up, hanging out with his two little sisters, Kim and Stephanie, riding bikes all over town, and having fun.

I was in my senior year of high school when I moved in with them. In August 1986, it was Ms. Brenda who began the conversation about our future. What were we going to do with our lives after high school? What were our plans? I didn't have an answer, but what I did know was that I had big dreams of leaving Florida and seeing the world.

I didn't tell her that initially. One afternoon she cornered me in the kitchen and began giving me the usual speech of how I could be doing more with my life instead of just spending money and "running around out in them streets." Normally, Terry and I would be getting this speech together, but somehow, he was missing in action that day. I had heard it so often that I could repeat it. Then, under the radar, she slid in ten new words: "blah, blah, blah...because ***I see more in you than you see in yourself.***" Her voice and those words are forever engraved in my mind. They are a core memory, and I can confirm to you all these years later that she did, and man, was she right!

Once she finally had my undivided attention, she asked me what I wanted to do with my life. All I knew was that I wanted to get out of Florida to see the world and what it truly had to offer. Let me quote what every mother tells her children when they make an open-ended statement: "Be careful what you ask for!" Within a matter of hours, I found myself standing outside a United States Air Force Recruiting office. You see, Ms. Brenda knew what most young black boys didn't know back then (and unfortunately still don't know today): the fastest way out of Altamonte, at least for me, was through the military. I think the best thing we can do for our youth is let them see the world through their own eyes. The scariest thing my wife and I did for our son was send him on a European educational trip for two weeks. As nerve-racking as that was, his experiences there far outweighed our fears.

Discussing me attending college back then would have been a waste of time and conversation because no one was going to college in my neighborhood, and I was still heavily influenced by my neighborhood, and in particular, street life. The only way I would shift my mindset from dreaming of a life that I wanted to live to living the life I've always dreamed was to leave Altamonte, leave my comfort zone. Ms. Brenda was my moral conscience that made it happen for me. She didn't really care what branch I joined; she was simply determined to get me out of Florida and to see the world. I told her the Air Force interested me because Reg was in the Air Force, so off we went. Luckily for the Army, the Air Force Recruiting office was closed and apparently only open by appointment.

The short version of how I became a soldier involves the five words an Army recruiter eventually said to me. As I was walking past his office with plans to return the next day and join the Air Force, I heard, "Hey! You got a minute? Can I talk to you right quick? So why do you want to join the Air Force?"

"My brother is in the Air Force, so I'm just following in his footsteps."

"Well, what if I told you that ***you can outrank your brother?***"

"Outrank my brother?" I didn't really know what that meant, but it sounded to me like I could finally beat him at something.

"Where do I sign?" I asked.

My brother Reg is a huge inspiration in my life and my military career. I most definitely followed in his footsteps. When the recruiter painted that beautiful portrait of my victory over Reg the Ruler, how could I resist? I love my big brother, but a little sibling rivalry, in my opinion, is healthy for every family, and the rest, as they say, is history. Army Basic Training is full of inspirational and motivational words! Those of you who have been there know what I'm talking about; if you haven't, maybe you saw it on television. For the record, there is no reality TV show anyone could ever make that will come close. I'm talking about a life-altering process that creates a lifetime bond of brothers and sisters.

After weeks of paperwork and physicals and a three-month delay for me to graduate from high school, waiting for the next basic training class to start, I finally left behind my small town of Altamonte Springs, Florida. I arrived at the airport on December 1, 1987, anxious to board my flight. The reality of that moment hit me all at once as the plane left the ground and I could feel the wheels stowing away beneath me. My dreams were now reality. The boy in me had just gotten one step closer to becoming a man. It was hard saying goodbye to my hometown, but it was necessary.

Next stop, Birmingham, Alabama, home to Fort McClellan and headquarters for the Military Police and Chemical Corp. That was my first flight, and because it was a short one, I found out quickly why they call smaller planes "crop dusters." Here's some advice for you: If you've never flown in an airplane before, make sure your first flight is a jumbo jet.

Much of the process from Birmingham to there is a blur. I remember getting all my new clothes, signing my name, and writing my social security number God knows how many times. I will never forget my first Army haircut. I know for a fact that there are zero qualifications to becoming an Army barber! At the time I entered the Army, I had the most popular hairstyle of the 1980s — the infamous Jheri curl (thank you, Mr. Redding). If you know anything about this hairstyle, you know that you can't go twelve hours without your Jheri curl activator! I was well into a week without mine, and let's just say that Don King had nothing on me. This guy they called the barber had a field day with all the black guys coming in at that time — all big-time supporters of Mr. Redding! By the time he got to my head, cutting mohawks wasn't fun anymore, so he decided to cut mine sideways. There were a lot of tears in that shop that day, and I suspect all the days before and after.

I don't remember a lot of the words or processes from that time, but I do remember the long bus ride to Fort McClellan from the Military Entry Processing Station (MEPS), or "Freedom's Front Door," as it's often referred.

There we were, making the long-dreaded ride, not knowing what to expect when we arrived at the training site. I haven't heard that kind of silence since then. I remember arriving at the front gate and seeing, "Welcome to Fort McClellan, home of the Chemical Corps and Military Police."

After the bus stopped at our final resting place, a very nice man came onto the bus. He said some influential words that are still clear in my head. In a very calm voice, he said, "Privates, I'm Drill Sergeant Thompson and I want to welcome you to Fort McClellan, Alabama. I hope you had a smooth ride down here from Birmingham." Then, all hell broke loose. He screamed at the top of his voice, "NOW GET YOUR SORRY ASSES OFF MY BUS! YOU GOT THIRTY SECONDS FOR EVERY LAST ONE OF YOU SONS A BITCHES TO GRAB YOUR GEAR, GET OFF MY BUS, AND BE IN FORMATION NOW!"

None of us knew what the hell this possessed man was talking about, and we surely had no idea how to get into a formation. I remember just running around in circles, completely confused and fully understanding the real meaning of "shock and awe." That's when I heard the second set of words that resonated with me.

Life teaches us so many lessons, and we learn from people of all walks of life — take daycare or preschool, for instance. We've all been a participant in the game "follow the leader." We pretty much know what it means — we follow whoever is in the front. That's not exactly true in basic training; it's truly a win and lose situation. In basic training, it's not called follow the leader; it's called watch and learn from the first victim. This poor soul will either execute the command given by the drill sergeant correctly or fail miserably. It's our job to follow the leader when he's executed correctly. If not, we wait for the results from the next victim in line, all of us hoping that he will find the correct path to lead all of the class to the promise land (that mystical place where the drill sergeant isn't yelling at you and everyone is enjoying a cool breeze on a nice afternoon filled with zero stress and nothing but smiles).

After a series of failed executions of the drill sergeant's order, I heard him yell to one of the guys on the bus with me, "BEAT YOUR FACE!" I knew I was giving the confused, head-tilted-to-the-side puppy dog face, because I didn't understand what the hell this deranged guy was asking. Why would he want this guy to beat his face? Without wasting a second between the command and his response, the soldier started slapping himself in the face. The drill sergeant came out of character for a split second and began to laugh. When he regained his composure, he told the private to get down and give him 20 (everything is about push-ups in basic training) until he said to stop. We all now knew what "beat your face" meant.

That smirk, that look on his face, that attempt to hold back the laughter as this poor kid punched himself in the face was the moment when I saw the game. I had found a glitch in the matrix. That out-of-character moment put me at ease as I realized that although these were serious times, this was a game of words and results, and as long as I could deliver the results, I would win the game.

Later in my career, I would be introduced to the most profound words I had heard up to that point in my military career. I must admit that I hadn't given much attention to these words prior to being promoted to sergeant. It's part of the tradition of entering the ranks of the noncommissioned officer that you know the NCO creed. The first time I read the opening line, I was hooked and instantly sold on the possibilities: "***No One is More Professional than I.***" I knew from the moment I said it that it was written for me; it was very similar to Ms. Brenda speaking her words, "I see more in you than you see in yourself." It was so powerful that I instantly became focused on my next positions. I would always work two levels above the rank I am currently assigned.

"The Creed of the Noncommissioned Officer"

"No one is more professional than I. I am a noncommissioned officer, a leader of soldiers. As a noncommissioned officer, I realize that I am a member of a time-honored corps, which is known as "The Backbone of the Army." I am proud of the Corps of Noncommissioned Officers and will at all times conduct myself so as to bring credit upon the corps, the military service, and my country; regardless of the situation in which I find myself. I will not use my grade or position to attain pleasure, profit, or personal safety.

Competence is my watchword. My two basic responsibilities will always be uppermost in my mind: Accomplishment of my mission and the welfare of my soldiers. I will strive to remain technically and tactically proficient. I am aware of my role as a noncommissioned officer; I will fulfill my responsibilities inherent in that role. All soldiers are entitled to outstanding leadership; I will provide that leadership. I know my soldiers, and I will always place their needs above my own. I will communicate consistently with my soldiers, and never leave them uninformed. I will be fair and impartial when recommending both rewards and punishment.

Officers of my unit will have maximum time to accomplish their duties; they will not have to accomplish mine. I will earn their respect and confidence as well as that of my soldiers. I will be loyal to those with whom I serve; seniors, peers, and subordinates alike. I will exercise initiative by taking appropriate action in the absence of orders. I will not compromise my integrity, nor my moral courage. I will not forget, nor will I allow my comrades to forget that we are professionals, noncommissioned officers, leaders!"

Many times, it wasn't only what the person said that stuck with me; it was the actions they took after they said it. Being on my own in the military was my personal test and introduction to manhood. What I learned from it was that actions don't speak louder than words; they validate them.

After leaving Fort McClellan, I spent the next ninety days at Fort Rucker, Alabama, learning my military occupational specialty (MOS) and sharpening my skills in effectively communicating with my peers, while realizing the reality of my youth and either unfortunately or fortunately, maintaining a portion of mischief. From there, I would be assigned to my first duty station, which was Darmstadt, West Germany.

"Be careful what you ask for; you just might get it!" Remember that? From the suburbs of Orlando, Florida, to Europe in a matter of less than one year of me saying, and I quote, "I want to see the world," I was on my way. Before leaving for Germany, the Army granted me a few weeks of leave. I took full advantage of my vacation time with my family back in Altamonte Springs.

My insecurities as a child led me to believe that my mother didn't love me like I thought she should. I've since realized how wrong I was. I realized how proud of me she was when I caught her crying during my basic training graduation. The second time I saw her "proud mama pride" was my graduation from Advanced Individual Training (AIT), and that time her tears were purely from pride. I could be over-exaggerating this, but I could swear I saw her grinning from ear to ear, like a kid left all alone in a candy store. I'm sure she way saying to herself, "Look at my boy!"

There's nothing better than to see your mom in a proud mamma moment; it truly is priceless. The third time I saw that pride on her face was during my leave before heading for Germany. That's when she got to show me off to the other moms around the neighborhood, and I was happy to overemphasize the new and professional Sean to everyone.

Since my teenage years, I've always been the main character and life of the party to my mom. To be funny, I would purposefully address her by her first name, Anne, when I had a question or statement to make. One evening during my leave when we were alone, I walked over to her and hugged her around her neck with my right arm.

"Anne, are you proud of your baby boy?" I asked her. I'm not good at being sentimental, so this wasn't a solemn moment where I asked her in tears or from a vulnerable state. I can still see her face.

"Boy, you so crazy," she said with a shy Lomax (her maiden name) smirk. "Yes, I'm proud of you."

I really loved hearing those words. I'm reminded of what a good friend of mine once said: "Trust the process."

I wish I could tell every child in the process now to trust it. The only problem is that you won't know it until you're through it. You just have to hang in there and ask lots of crazy questions from time to time. My mom loved soap operas. She was a "Young and the Restless" fanatic, as well as "General Hospital" (back when Luke and Laura were the talk of the town). She didn't talk like the people on those soap operas, where everyone's words were filled with emotion and passion. Neither do I, but all of our emotional conversations, were far greater than any soap opera moment. They were our soap opera moments.

I was excited to be leaving for Germany. It was my first time flying over any ocean — the Atlantic Ocean at that! Flying across the Atlantic Ocean is as close as one can get to time travel. I lost a day getting over there and gained one coming home.

I was a week into my new home for the next two years and just getting adjusted to my new surroundings when I received a phone call with news that wrecked my world. Stephanie, the daughter of Uncle Clifford and Aunt Dorothy, had passed away. Our families were so close that anyone would have thought that the Angrys and Jacksons were the same family. Stephanie was my first cousin, but she was more than that. I thought of her as my little sister. We did so much together as kids. Every summer, you would see Terry, Kim, Stephanie, and me somewhere in town together. Those really were the good ole days.

When I received the news of her death, I was completely numb. I remember walking through the halls of the headquarters building in Darmstadt around 9 o'clock in the morning and hearing a voice yell, "PVT Angry, how are you doing?" It was my company commander, Major Emil F. Meiz. I can't recall exactly what I said, but it was short and to the point.

All I wanted to do after getting the news was to get home, but that didn't seem possible. I was a private on my first duty assignment and I didn't have a wealthy family, so I knew I wasn't getting on a plane to go back across the Atlantic without the Army's support. I had received Red Cross briefings and knew that since Stephanie wasn't an immediate family member, the Red Cross really couldn't help or support me in getting home.

The next words out of his mouth instilled in me another true value of results-driven leadership. He stopped a sergeant (E-5) that was walking by and gave him a direct order to drop whatever he was doing and take me everywhere I needed to go to ensure I was on the next flight home to be with my family. He told him to report back to him when he was done. He wanted me out of the country by the end of the day, but through no fault of his own, the sergeant couldn't make that happen. I will say that he was diligent and determined to accomplish his mission. Even when we encountered the occasional, "He can't do that," the sergeant made it happen. I was home with my family the following day.

That's the kind of leader I'm going to be, I told myself in the middle of everything going on.

3

Mentors

"We can be knowledgeable with other men's knowledge, but we can't be wise with other men's wisdom."

Montaigne

DURING MY TENURE as the Army National Guard's Equal Opportunity sergeant major in 2004, I would travel to each state conducting sensing sessions of the program and how it was working for the command. I had the opportunity to sit with a National Guard soldier during one of my program assessment visits. What initially caught my eye was the age of the soldier. He was an older gentleman and when I asked his age, he told me 65. Why that caught my attention was that he was only an E-5 sergeant. It was so odd to me because the company first sergeant was still in his twenties.

I asked the soldier the obvious question: "Why are you still an E-5?"

I was taken aback by his response: "I'm just trying to make it through the gauntlet."

He explained to me that there were two standards within his company. Certain people were given mentors, provided guidance and opportunities, while others were left to figure it out on their own, thus surviving the gauntlet. At that very moment, my life flashed back over my career; I saw all the faces of people who were there for me, to mentor, guide, and teach me what I knew then. Mentors are the single most important ingredient to a successful life, whether that success is a career in the military, raising a family, or being the best person you can be.

There was a wealth of knowledge at my fingertips. Utilizing this valuable resource was the key to my success and provided me guidance, direction, motivation, and self-actualization: "What a man can be, he must be" (Maslow, A). I heard it said so much in my young career that mentors select the mentee, basically giving no say in the decision to the mentee. I believe there is fifty percent truth to that statement; the other fifty lies with the individual seeking mentors. I'm very grateful for my mentors who decided to invest the time in developing me into the leader I am today. I call each of them my silent heroes, because even to this day, none of them seek recognition for my success. I've also met leaders and individuals whose lifestyles impressed me so much that I had to have them join my A team; even to this day, their counsel is unwavering. I've also learned throughout my career that not every mentor has good intentions as a mentor. That's why I'm not one hundred percent sold on the statement that mentors select their mentees only. I've had so-called mentors with ulterior motives that weren't good fits for my career, and as negative hidden agendas go, they were only good for theirs. I think hidden agendas can be a good thing when achieving them positively affects the whole.

It's equally true that when you see something you like in a person, you should respectfully ask if they wouldn't mind being on your team — your mentorship team. I've had times in my young career where certain leaders would thrust themselves into my life, telling me they were going to mentor me. That never worked out as intended. True leadership doesn't work that way to me. A true leader, in my opinion, is what I call a silent mentor. A person who gives you what you need, watches you grow and mature, and never once thrusts themselves upon you or seeks credit for your improvements.

Mentors like MSG (Ret.) Miriam Wallace, who reminded me of Ms. Brenda, beginning when I was a young specialist (E-4). She saw better in me and wanted it from me while I was under her leadership; I admired her leadership style and how adversity seemed to simply roll off her back. This was during a time in the Army when adversity wasn't the buzz word of the military and not something in the forefront. She took care of company business, and I never saw an issue where her race or gender was used as an excuse by her or someone used it against her. She was a very solid and professional leader.

An interesting thing about my mentors is that early in my Army career they all sought me out. Many times it was because of a disciplinary issue or tightening up on my "being on time to formations" issue. It wasn't until I led troops that I began to seek out others I felt could help me to grow and better myself as a leader. Being placed in charge was comfortable for me, and because of it I didn't want to fail at it, so I began to seek out leaders I felt could help me grow and provide me a safety net in case I did fall. Failure wasn't an option for me, and where others failed in seeking guidance, I used it as a source for my success. I also began to take the good things I saw in leaders and add them to my leadership bag to improve myself at every opportunity.

I've been very fortunate in my military career to meet some great soldiers and civilians who without question joined my A-team of advisors. John Tilley is one of these advisors. I met 1st Sgt. (Ret.) Tilley on my tour of duty at Fort Belvoir, Virginia, with further assignment to Davison Army Airfield, assigned to the Centralized Army Aviation Support Office (CAASO) from 1990 to 1992. I knew from the first time he saw me and the look he had on his face that he was going to be one of those leaders who wouldn't sugarcoat what he had to say, and he would expect nothing but the best from me. Sure enough, that's exactly what he expected and demanded.

"Why do you have that on your window? Can it be any bigger? What does it mean?" He was referring to the large red letters stamped across the back window of my red 1989 Nissan Sentra that I purchased brand new while I was stationed in Germany. I didn't know it at that time, but I was learning from him how to identify with myself and developing my brand of who I was. I was learning the difference between being a leader and a follower. At that time, I was surely a follower, like most young people were back then and many are today. That wasn't necessarily a bad thing, but running around town with a rearview window that displayed the word NASTY in large bold red letters more than likely wasn't going to get me the attention that I wanted. Nasty Nissan was a car club that a few of us with

Nissans had come up with for attention, only it wasn't the right attention for a destined military career soldier to be seeking.

He didn't order me to remove it from my car — that's not the type of leader he was. He continued to coach and mentor me over the next few months. The more I began to lean towards leading, the more I could distinguish between the negative attention my car brought me and the professional attention I represented. It was only then that I made the decision to remove the letters from my car and began focusing on my destiny. Some of the greatest leaders of my time have prepared me for leadership. All my experiences with them prepared me for the opportunity I was presented when I was asked to fill in as the interim command sergeant major of the Army National Guard.

I was more than confident that I could do the job, and even excel in it. My first day on the job, sitting behind the desk of the highest ranking enlisted in the Guard, I knew the next move I made would be critical, and so that move was to create my council of advisors. Honestly, I didn't have much senior leader support in the building, nor in the entire Army Guard at that time, frankly, because of how everything leading up to that point occurred. I reached out to someone I had spent a little time with earlier in my Guard career who always had solid advice for me as I advanced through the Army National Guard: Command Sgt. Maj. (Ret.) John Leonard, who was also a former command sergeant major of the Army National Guard. Because of how I assumed command, I didn't have a lot of time for briefings and to get brought up to speed on the direction of the Army Guard in mid stride. Honestly, I liked it that way; I've always worked better inside of chaos. I reached out to him and asked him, "If you could do it all over again, what is the one thing you would do differently?" I then told him that I was now the interim command sergeant major of the Guard.

He was very happy to hear from me and extremely happy to hear this news. He quickly congratulated me, saying it was the right answer for the Guard, given the circumstances. He proceeded to tell me that he would've relied more on his advisors and that I should contact certain personnel that still worked in the building. They were Sgt. Maj. (Ret.) Joyce Bull and Sgt. Maj. (Ret.) Tom McNamara, gurus of Army National Guard Readiness Center (ARNGRC — the headquarters building for the Army National Guard) policy and history. I also added Sgt. Maj. (Ret.) Gary Robinson to my advisory council, as he was an initial mentor of mine during my tour as the Equal Opportunity sergeant major.

By taking John's advice, I successfully maneuvered through a period in the Army National Guard that was as fragile as any situation I had faced in my career. You are never too old to seek advice and counsel, and only a fool thinks they know it all. I knew instantly to put my foolish ways behind me. Mentors are a critical part of the development of not only your career, but also of your life. Although giving up is not in my DNA, given the circumstances and the challenges I faced with many leaders I represented, I don't think I could have successfully fulfilled my obligation if it wasn't for my advisors and mentors. Each of them proved to be invaluable to me and still are today.

I would be remiss if I didn't mention a critical mentor of mine at the peak moment in my career, Sergeant Major of the Army Kenneth O. Preston. As one command sergeant major put it during my first meeting to Preston's advisory council, "CSM Angry has been handed a shit sandwich."

Trust me, as much fun as I had managing and maintaining that level of chaos, his comment was an understatement. What I immediately admired about Preston was that he instantly saw me. What I mean by that is everything I said earlier about my belief in myself, that I was meant to be in in the highest level of leadership, he saw in me as well. Either that or like great leaders do, he gave me the benefit of the doubt and provided a training wheel as a precautionary measure until he saw that I could ride on my own. Whichever it was, his council was key to my success during this interim period. I'm very appreciative of the time he took out of his very busy schedule to answer my questions and provide me with guidance I needed to perform my duties as the CSM of the Army National Guard.

There were two moments in our interactions as leaders when I felt that he understood my challenges. The first occurred during our annual Enlisted Association of the National Guard of the United States (EANGUS) Conference where he's routinely invited to speak. Prior to his arrival, like any effective leader, I was brought up to speed on the behind-the-scene discussions of should Command Sergeant Major Angry be representing the office and position of CSM of the Army National Guard at this meeting? I was already involved in a few pressing issues and didn't plan to give this discussion any validity. It was always my intent to not only attend the conference but also to attend it as the command sergeant major of the Army National Guard as that was my official title, regardless of a status of acting or interim. He was introduced to speak to the junior and senior leaders who were in the audience, as well as the Army and Air National Guard leadership. What he said next was the instant I saw him. He began addressing the audience with a story of a soldier who at a young age went into the Civil War battle and performed very well in command. He performed so well that he was brevetted to brigadier general at the age of twenty-three, less than a week before the Battle of Gettysburg, where he personally led cavalry charges that prevented Confederate cavalry from attacking the Union rear in support of Pickett's Charge.

The soldier he was referring to was General Custer, who was present at General Robert E. Lee's surrender to General Ulysses S. Grant on April 9, 1865. The present-day soldier he referred to in that story was me. I believe it was a call to chance, an attempt to slow down the efforts of resistance and give the newly appointed leader a shot at leading. I don't think many in the room knew what that story was referencing, and if they did, it was never shared with me. I did thank the SMA for sharing the story and made sure he knew that I fully understood the importance and timing of it.

A large part of leadership involves asking direct and focused questions. Six months into my position as the interim CSM, I had the fortunate opportunity to be in the company of the Army's top three senior enlisted leaders: SMA Ken Preston (thirteenth sergeant major of the Army), CSM Marvin Hill (CSM of the 101st Airborne Division), and CSM Jeffrey Mellinger (CSM U.S. Army Material Command) during an event in Washington, D.C. At that time, in 2009, we were fighting two wars and beginning the planning phase to exit from Iraq while entering our eighth year in Afghanistan.

It was becoming increasingly noticeable to me that we were quickly shifting to a "what's on you" Army, instead of what's inside you. Combat badges, ribbons, and patches had become a "must have at any cost" item for the new definition of success. Here I was sitting with three distinguished leaders whose leadership styles and abilities were recognized by the most senior leader to the most junior soldier not for what was on them, but clearly by what's in them. Each had sound and proven counsel and a presence about them that commanded respect. I was in a unique situation with regard to my new position as the CSM for the Army National Guard since I wasn't assigned to the position because of my awards and decorations on my uniform. Now, with our current combat environment, badges were as visible as ever.

While I had their attention and mentorship guidance, I asked this distinguished group,

"Should I seek an assignment into theater, and if so, where would I best help the warfight?" I went on to explain that I didn't want to be a part of the big boy negative gossip (yes, there's a rumor mill even at the highest levels). I had heard passed-down comments of leaders' concern for personnel arriving into the theater of operation not being a part of the solution, but of the problem. Personnel were arriving into combat to receive combat awards and patches. Each of them agreed that I did need an assignment into theater. Each of them also agreed that I needed the right assignment and going over just for a patch wasn't the right answer. I couldn't have agreed more.

A few months after I was assigned as the interim command sergeant major, my new schedule took me to the annual Army Ten-Miler (ATM) to motivate the troops and all runners prior to race day. The ATM is the United States Army's premier and largest ten-mile road race, which starts and finishes at the Pentagon. It's tradition that the CSM of the Army National Guard and the Army Reserve join the SMA the evening prior to race day at the pasta dinner to eat and speak to the runners. This would be my first time crossing paths with Command Sgt. Maj. Leon Caffie, the Army Reserve's CSM.

I don't know if the lineup was based on position of service, seniority, or age, but I like to think it was age, since I spoke last. The SMA spoke first and gave a very good historic speech (he's an excellent speaker of history and facts). Then it was Caffie's turn, and my God! If you've ever heard this man speak, you know the emphasis and power he delivers to a crowd. Let me remind you that this was for self-inflicted pain for runners who voluntarily signed up to run, yet his words made every runner want to take the hill! It's nearly impossible to follow a speaker of his caliber, and that's exactly what I said before I shared a personal story of why I run: for my mother who passed away some years earlier. After that event, I sought out the counsel of Leon Caffie. I'm proud to say that far into both of our retired lives, we are still great friends.

I have three special Michelles in my world (they don't all spell their name the same way). The first is my wife, Michelle Ray. She's spent all her adult life educating our young people and future leaders. She reminds me so much of my mother who, like Michelle, never put herself before her children. She sacrificed most of her personal life ensuring we had every opportunity to enjoy and learn in ours. She's a silent community contributor and is a direct humanitarian.

The second Michelle is the greatest first lady America has had in leadership in my lifetime, Michelle Obama. Like my mother and my wife, Michelle has been an instrumental contributor to the success and motivation of so many of our youth.

I want to tell you about the third woman with this name in greater detail because she was an instrumental mentor of mine during my tenure as command sergeant major. She is Michele Jones, who was the ninth command sergeant major of the Army Reserve. I first crossed paths with her in 2005 while I was the sergeant major for the Army National Guard Equal Opportunity. She was invited to speak at our annual conference that year. Her speec was so motivating that I really wished I could have had a one-to-one conversation with her on her leadership philosophy and the challenges she faced in her career, and if God would have it, seek her counsel as a mentor. I remember sitting at home, after a hard day of holding an enlisted program together with all its pros and cons, watching the Democratic National Convention on television. Out on stage walked now retired Command Sgt. Maj. Michele S. Jones to introduce the Democratic Party nominee for president of the United States, candidate Barack Obama.

I knew at that moment that I had to have her on my council, so I reached out to her, congratulated her on all her continued accomplishments, and gave her the good news of my promotion. She was more than ecstatic and told me that if there was ever anything I needed, she was there for me and happy to help. I told her of my initial challenges and that I recalled her sharing similar challenges in her speech in 2005 and wanted to know how she approached dealing with them. She gave me some much-needed advice. She was true to her word in 2009, and I'm honored to say that nine years later she remains true to them. I recently had a situation I felt was so disrespectful that it brought me out of character, which violated my personal motto of professionalism. That is, "He who angers you conquers you." Once I realized what had occurred, I made it my priority to reach out to my experts and personal council. Michele offered some key insights and shared some stories of how she overcame a few situations in her career, which helped me significantly in understanding mine. I'm very appreciative of her guidance and mentorship, and more importantly, I'm thankful for her friendship.

Being a mentor is just as important to me as being mentored. I believe in the saying "pay it forward" and take every opportunity to help guide a career and offer insight to anyone seeking it whenever and wherever available. It goes back to the previous chapter on words, where I've expressed how the Creed of the Noncommissioned Officer changed my life and my leadership style:

"All soldiers are entitled to outstanding leadership; I will provide that leadership. I know my soldiers, and I will always place their needs above my own."

Some of them know they need leadership and others do not. That's why their needs are always placed above mine. Rising leaders like my cousin, Sergeant 1st Class Cleveland Taylor, who was recently promoted from staff sergeant. He asked many questions over his career and I gave him many answers. Now his next level of authority has caught up to him, leading him into the upper echelons of a senior NCO. Leaders like SGM Sean Baker, who worked under my leadership as a staff sergeant and is currently the SGM of the Office of Inspector General. There are so many more I can name here, but I will have to give an honorary mention to everyone I had the honor to assist and serve with by saying thank you for what you've accomplished, thank you for allowing me the opportunity to be a part of your growth, and as my friend CSM Traylor put it, "Thank you for trusting the process."

4

Fitness

"Outer strength is often a reflection of something stronger inside."

Unknown

I THINK FITNESS and leadership go together. I say this because to be fit requires focus — the focus to improve your body and how to perform better under pressure. This in turn instills discipline, which is a required characteristic of a good leader. The Army gave me that. The closest I came to fitness growing up was the public school system's version of physical fitness (PT). It was part of the school's curriculum that I compare to the very little I know about prison through my "as seen on television" experience of the inmates given time in the yard.

School fitness wasn't very organized. Basically, it was a field full of kids throwing a ball, running around a track, or for those who the coaches didn't see any athletic future in, sitting on and under the bleachers simply wasting time — something I never want to waste. Fitness instilled in me my never-give-up attitude. It helped me achieve both physical and mental toughness, which I use to push myself through the pain and be victorious! Yeah, I know winning isn't everything, but when I'm battling myself, winning is the only thing. It helped me to become a better leader and help others become victorious in their own lives. I believe that's a primary responsibility of leaders.

Fitness taught me that if I could push through a two-minute push-up and sit-up drill, give it all I had on a two-mile run to meet a specific time standard, and do those things well under the allotted time or minimum amount required to pass (although I always strived for the maximum), then as a leader or the one in charge, I could motivate others to do the same. Later in my career when I was a more seasoned and experienced leader, my troops would always hear me say, "Real leaders lead from the front." I believed (and still believe) that I had to be better than any of my soldiers, mentally and physically. I'm not saying this out of arrogance or to be cocky. I hold myself to very high standards, because I don't have a middle ground within myself. If I'm not striving and pushing myself to be the best that I can be, then the only thing

I will be is my worst. I've always believed that for anyone to be their best, they must see what being your best looks like. When it came to fitness, I wanted to instill a personal attitude of excellence in everyone under my command, and I would challenge them on many occasions.

The military brought out the competitor in me, and leadership taught me how to use my competitiveness to bring out the best in those under my watch. I love seeing others improve physically and mentally! During my time as the command sergeant major of the Operational Support Airlift Command (OSACOM), I put out a challenge that whoever could beat my time running the airfield would have my parking spot for a month along with "the Man or Woman" bragging rights forever, if they maintained the course title. Every morning, at 0530, you could drive past me running the airfield. On company PT mornings, you could catch me running into the 0600 formation just as the first sergeant was yelling, "Fall in." That morning ritual was a necessity to ensure my day was always a good one. My commander, Col. Michael Bishop, had a similar ritual, but instead of a first-light morning run, he would run the airfield every day at noon, like clockwork.

Tony Robbins said, "What separated Michael Phelps from his competition was the quality of his rituals." He went on to talk about how much more he outworked his competition to make himself better. In his case, Phelps was committed to his workout to produce results that made him better than the rest of his swimming competition to ensure he fulfilled his quest of winning the gold medal in the Olympics. His commitment to his rituals to become the greatest swimmer also made him a more disciplined person. Although I didn't list discipline as one of my principles, make no mistake, it's the root of them all.

Bishop's ritual and mine of running the airfield was a strong part of our daily routine. While we never directed any soldier to run with us at those hours, our commitment to that ritual created a new standard in helping them develop theirs. I would get weekly updates about who came close to beating my time, but I'm not a second-place trophy sergeant major and gave out no cheers for closeness — you either break the record or keep training until you do.

The challenge became a really good motivator for the command, which I wasn't expecting. The airfield is exactly 3.2 miles long and very scenic. It ran in a complete circle, with about half a mile hard road and the rest off-road or asphalt running.

The day came when it was time to pass the torch. I got the call that SSG Hyland Trent had broken my airfield record; not only did he break it, but he also shattered it! The time to beat was 18:30 and Trent ran it in 17:45 — that's less than a six-minute mile!

What I learned from that experience was that disciplined fitness is contagious. Our airfield runs were the fuel the troops needed to see, and the challenge was the spark that ignited it. Our ritual wasn't something we force-fed on the command; it was an unwritten discipline that ignited it. Physical fitness was a ritual that was forced on me early in my military career. The difference was that in the beginning it was mandatory, and I did it because leaders appointed over me directed it. Later in my career, fitness became a way of life for me, and I needed it to start my day off positively. It became a major part of me and the ritual to start my day. I would use my morning runs to organize my thoughts, so naturally, the length of my runs was a clue as to how organized my thoughts were, and as a self-diagnosed Organizational Compulsive Disorder candidate, I had to get them in order.

This was especially true for a period of my life when my mind was absolutely unorganized, and running took on a new meaning. On May 22, 2001, almost at the height of my military career, the unexpected occurred. My mother passed away. I was a company first sergeant of the Hawaii Regional Flight Center stationed at Hickam Air Force Base, Hawaii. I was well into a successful career. I had broken through many of the glass ceilings and had proven myself as a leader of soldiers.

I've always looked at my life as a puzzle. The challenges and struggles I overcame were the pieces that fell into place. My mom was the wizard who would give me the clues to my life whenever I stumbled. These clues were the keys to what piece of the puzzle I would pick up next. Before she died, the puzzle showed a picture of my life I was absolutely loving. All my hard work, discipline, and commitment had paid off.

I was a young, successful African American first sergeant (E-8), rising through the military ranks. I had a beautiful family, no debt, and lived on beautiful Oahu, Hawaii, with the sky my only limit.

When she died, I felt like I died with her. I was completely lost. That puzzle was nearly complete, a thousand pieces in place. Now, the picture was destroyed, all the pieces scattered or lost.

I didn't know how I would return to Hawaii. I had so many responsibilities as a husband, a father, and a first sergeant, and I didn't know how I would return to lead any of them. Everything seemed too difficult. I couldn't think about much of anything. I didn't want to do anything. I didn't know how I would find myself again.

I was a real wreck. I had to figure things out quickly if I was going to survive this. So I went back to the beginning. I redefined my foundation and purpose, which had been so strong through all these years. I realized that my core had stayed true to who I am and have aspired to be. What I was overlooking through all of this was my love of running and how it cleared my mind. Once I realized my serenity in running, I started running again. I eventually entered a 10k race that ran along the beach of Waikiki. I didn't realize I had won it until I heard cheering as I crossed the finish line.

I thought about my mom the entire run. I didn't call it a race because I wasn't focused on the runners — only my mother and how I was going to get my life back together without her. That race began the reorganization process in my head, and I needed a lot more time on the road to make progress. I continued running every day after that race; as the miles got longer, the puzzle once again began coming together. Thirteen marathons later, I have made great progress. A psychiatrist once told me that I've been running from my mother's death, and I'm completely OK with that.

5

Tenacity

"No matter how tall the mountain is, it cannot block the sun. Tenacity and adversity are old foes."

Chinese Proverb

I THINK THE hardest thing to be in life is yourself. When I was growing up, my family and everyone in the neighborhood called me by my middle name, Sean. My mom's favorite actor in the world was Sean Connery, so that's how I got the name. However, my family and neighborhood didn't pronounce it "Shawn" as he did. They pronounced it like "Seen" or "Scene," with a long "e" and no "h" sound.

I love me some "Seen" despite all his insecurities and flaws. My biggest fear in those days was growing up, getting older, and losing myself to becoming someone else through all the peers and pressures of life. You know that inner child everyone talks about? He fought to stay alive on this journey, and I'd like to let you know that he made it. I wasn't always happy with my life. There were days growing up when I felt that if I had to classify myself, I would be a below-average kid who had a lot of dreams in his head and no way of getting them out. I lived in my head growing up and dealt with the world as it was presented to me every day.

I can see Seen's face now as I think back to a day in the year 1978, when I was ten years old. I can distinctly remember lying in bed thinking about my life as an adult. What would I be in life? Would anyone ever fall in love with me? Would I ever have a family? Would I even make it to being an adult? I thought about death a lot in those days; I just wasn't sure about anything in my life back then.

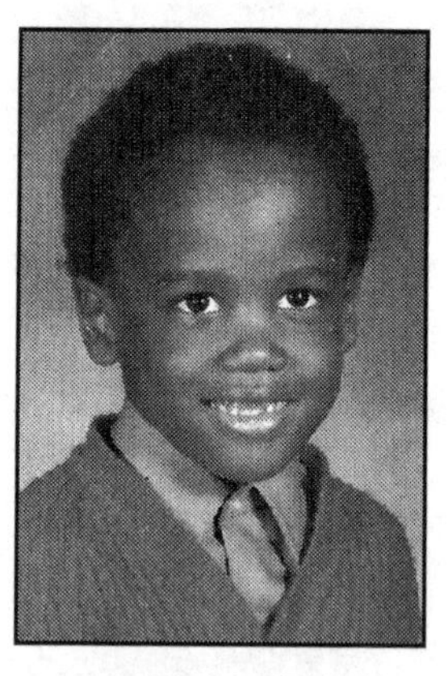

There are a lot of constants in life, and one of them is that change is inevitable and a necessity. I've had many great successes in my life, from getting married; having beautiful children, nieces, and nephews; and a very successful military career. My innermost personal success, though, is that I brought myself with me through it all. Like the scene from the blockbuster movie "Hook," where the "lost boy" is trying to validate if the adult man, Peter (Robin Williams), is really the lost boy, Peter Pan. It's a really cute scene of how easily influenced children are; it ends with one kid believing that the adult Peter is also Peter Pan, just buried deep inside him. It's only when he pulls adult Peter's cheeks back to his ears that he finds young Peter Pan and says, "Oh, there you are, Peter!" I really connected with that "scene" (pun intended).

It was 1987, while I was in Army Basic Training, when I first realized I was good at the leadership position. My class and I had been together for about a month and had already broke through our biases, judgments, and fears of each other and were now functioning as a team. Class leaders were assigned and had a life expectancy of one week before being "killed off" and replaced by a new person on the spot: "PVT Angry, PVT Gilley is dead, and you are in charge now." That was that — you were either ready for it or died within a few hours of being promoted. I never thought of myself as a quick learner. School was a challenge for me; I was labeled as a slow learner and attended slow learner classes called the "Super Team" from sixth to eighth grades.

When I was growing up, children weren't diagnosed with Attention Deficit Disorder (ADD), at least not in my community. It wasn't until recent years that I learned I didn't have a learning disability; I just needed to find a way to make whatever I was a part of interesting to me. Leading people to influence them to accomplish a mission was very interesting to me. It gained all my attention as I watched others process how they were going to fulfill that task — and watched so many of them fail. Many of the steps outlined in this book are what I learned in basic training. What I learned personally through that experience was that I was growing and becoming an upgraded version of myself, an evolution of Sean, and like the good book says, "To whom much has been given, much will be required" (Luke 12:48).

Being placed in leadership positions did so much for my career and life. Leadership really helped shape the man I am today. It's so much more than influencing others; it's becoming intricately involved with their lives and their problems up close and very personal. I learned a term at the Defense Equal Opportunity Management Institute (DEOMI) that I would use daily in my interactions with people: Significant Emotional Event (SEE). My problem has always been that I'm very organized, and I transferred simple things like organizing my desk (which had a blueprint to where everything was located) to organizing people. I would get so consumed in repairing their problems that if I wasn't sad with them,

I would be angry at them and asking myself, *Why would someone do this to themselves, and how do I get them out of it?*

Mind you that this isn't a recommended characteristic of a leader, because it can get costly, not only in time and resources but in money as well. Here's some valuable information to anyone rising through the leadership ranks: There's a reason you don't lend money to any troop in a difficult situation. In my experience, you'll go broke doing it! I was told this early in my leadership career, as I'm sure his mentor told him, and so on.

The textbook answer is that it's not a leader's responsibility to provide monetary assistance to a subordinate's SEE. It's the leader's responsibility to be aware of the many programs in place to assist a person in need and to connect them with those organizations. That's not to say that in many of my interactions where I was overly involved in situations, those individuals weren't appreciative of my support and genuine concern for their success. It's to say that there's a very thin line to ride when you find yourself too involved.

That thin line is referenced in Maslow's Hierarchy of Needs, riding between *Esteem needs: Prestige and feeling of accomplishment* and *Belongingness and love needs: Intimate relationships and friends*. I was obsessed with accomplishment and creating belongingness for myself, as well as wanting everyone on my team to belong. One of my catch phrases you could hear echoing through the halls was, "There are no friends in the military!" That's not entirely true, but it was a statement I'd make when soldiers tried to cover for someone when one of them was in trouble (like I hadn't done that before in my younger career).

In fact, on the very smallest scale, I wanted everyone in the command to be friends. Friendship is such a risky statement to use in the military, because nothing should ever override professionalism, and it's that which makes the military great. The ability to always do what's right no matter the level of connection to an individual, a group, or even family, and that is by far the hardest thing to do! I think for me, Col. (Ret.) Fred Chesbro said it best: "When I go to the car lot to buy a car, the salesman comes out trying really hard to be my friend, and I don't need him to be my friend. I need him to sell me a car." To paraphrase: When in charge, be in charge! It comes with easy decisions on some days and very hard, complex decisions on others. When it came to taking care of others, especially in their Significant Emotional Event, the inner part of me wanted to be the neutralizer. "Seen" didn't have the training for that, but he had the tenacity to let his sun shine through.

In 1989, when I was twenty-one years old, one of my greatest mentors, then SFC John Tilley, had invested a lot of time developing me. I was short in the growth and maturity department. I was a huge supporter of the advancement of hip hop, which began to catch the government's attention because of groups like Public Enemy and N.W.A. (Niggaz with Attitudes), who had released the most controversial rap at that time, "F**k the Police." I was a young black man torn between two worlds, as those were the days when young black men were referred to as "Super Predators," a term coined by then President Ronald Reagan and heavily supported by politicians all over. I mention this because in those days it really was a proud feeling to be black in America, and in my case, serving my country.

Although I didn't truly know what that meant at the time, it just felt good being accepted by "white people." That's not being in any way disrespectful. It was a serious feeling I had as a young man back then; unfortunately, today I can see my younger self in the attitudes of a lot of young black men. I was facing my biggest character challenge in my young military career, and that was preserving my identity and never forgetting where I came from. During those days, I would say that I was about forty percent confident in myself and was still influenceable. I wanted what every young black kid wanted then: to be accepted and acknowledged for all those things I was doing for my country.

My worst encounter with racism came in 1990 while I was home on leave and spent the day with my mom, driving her around town running errands. That's when I noticed the police car in my rearview mirror. My heart rate instantly increased, and I told my mom there was a policeman behind us. She didn't think anything of it and said, "You haven't done anything wrong."

When his emergency lights came on, I really began freaking out. Profiling was not a thought in the eighties, and minority rights was a joke. I hated that I was about to go through the normal drill of being pulled over, because my mom was in the car and I hated that she had to see that crap. Even worse, I was afraid that the police officer would be one of the extra assholes who would pull her out of the car and subject her to his bullshit procedures. Thankfully, he wasn't the super asshole — just an asshole — so I was greatly relieved.

My mother only had to sit in the car as he made me exit the vehicle and stand to the rear. He searched me, looked through my car, and then made me stand there as he sat in his car, staring me in the eyes as he "ran my plates" and my identification. Since I was now in the military, I thought that giving him my identification card would gain me the respect of being excused from this harassment, but I was wrong. Thirty minutes later, he finally stepped out of his car, telling me that there was a report of a stolen car matching the description of mine. Nothing on his face looked sincere or gave me the impression that he was telling the truth, and the reality was that I knew that line was standard procedure.

It wasn't the first time myself or any of the fellas in my neighborhood had heard it, and it wouldn't be the last. If you listen to the lyrics of NWA's controversial song, you will hear a lot of similarities in my story. Ice Cube sums it up best when he says, "thinking every nigger is selling narcotics" and "a young nigga got it bad cause he's brown." I hated that experience, not for me but for my mother. She was very proud of my military career and saw the positive direction my life was going; she saw the man I would eventually become even back then, and I hated that she had to witness that experience so much that I wanted to cry! We didn't say much when I got back into the car and drove off. I just wanted to forget that ever happened and continue moving in the right direction, and making her happy and proud of me.

That was a defining moment of tenacity for me. I made a promise to myself that I would never be ashamed of my ethnicity, my heritage, or my race, no matter the cost. If a person or group did not like me for the color of my skin, they would have to deal with it, because if there was one thing I was sure of, it was that I was going places and no ignorant human being would get in the way of my destiny.

6

Preparation

"Luck and timing is a short list of professionals who have prepared themselves to be on it."

Lt. Gen (R) Gregory Biscone

I PREPARED MYSELF by focusing on four key areas: 1: Giving the credit to those who truly deserved it. 2: Remaining in the positive light (being visible). 3: Taking the "unpopular" assignments. 4: Fully understand the Beast!

In 1992, I was the operations noncommissioned officer for the 4th Battalion, 501st Attack Aviation Battalion stationed at Camp Page, Korea. The company was going through an Aviation Resource Management Survey (ARMS) inspection. Anyone who has ever been through one will tell you that it's a grueling process to prepare for, and this was my first in my new career. One of my greatest strengths, and weakness, is my OCD and need for perfection, which came through when the inspection was concluded. We passed with all high markings and commendable comments so good that leadership held an awards ceremony to honor everyone involved in ensuring we not only passed, but also excelled better than our other three companies and two other battalions. Normally awards ceremonies are conducted during the battalion formation once a month, but because of the significance of the ARMS results there was a special ceremony held for the operations team.

The narrator read the write-up, which talked about the attention to detail that goes into successfully passing an ARMS inspection on the first evaluation and the preparation that goes into ensuring perfection. My section had worked very hard to ensure that every record was flawless, with zero mistakes. It was an attention to detail that came natural to me. I've been an organizer all my life. As the names were called, one by one each person went to receive their Army Achievement Medal (AAM). After the last medal was pinned, the commander called for a round of applause for all the recipients.

As I stood there applauding them for their award, my team looked over at me in disbelief. I was the young E-5 who had carried the command through a first-time, exceptional rating of an ARMS inspection. I was in total shock, and I knew I couldn't outwardly show it. At that moment, I made a critical decision in my career: I would get in this game (line of work) for the soldier and not for myself! I knew at that moment that this would happen again, and that if I didn't decide then how I would control my destiny, it would control me. I tried convincing myself that it was just an oversight of management and that someone would correct it later.

My soldiers and KATUSA (Korean Augmentation to the United States Army) began to be insubordinate with facial expressions and a few negative comments directed at leadership as to why I wasn't presented an award. I wanted to show what good leadership was and made it a direct point to place them at ease (a military command used to silence a soldier and have them give the person who called it their undivided attention).

That was also the first time I had seen my worth defended by a group of people outside of family members. That one act alone showed me the value I brought to my team, and it was a wonderful feeling of accomplishment for me. I lost a lot of good battle buddies who left the Army once they reached their Expiration of Term of Service (ETS) because of the failures of leadership to properly recognize their accomplishments or simply say thank you.

It was about this time in 1993 that I ran across the quote, "He who angers you conquers you" (Elizabeth Kenny). To be conquered is to be defeated, and I didn't join the Army to be defeated by anyone, not even myself. The way I saw it, if I could make it through the wrath of Ms. Brenda and a pair of crazy drill sergeants, everyone else was simply a walk in the park.

Once I understood the Army culture and how to progress through its system of promotion and positions, I was completely obsessed with excelling in it. CT Fletcher (bodybuilder and social media and YouTube fitness celebrity) calls it a "Magnificent Obsession" — that thing you love doing so much that it totally consumes you as you strive to perfect it. His is bodybuilding; mine is leadership. Influencing others to achieve a common goal, which is to accomplish the mission, any mission, was my true passion. I really enjoyed the team-building process. When I got teams to operate together to achieve the military goal, it was even more exciting to watch individuals win personal battles within themselves that strengthen their loyalty to the organization and its goals.

Being a member of a time-honored corps known as the backbone of the Army became my magnificent obsession. I wanted to be the best that I could be in it. One major thing I discovered about myself in basic training was that I'm very competitive. Once I discovered how to will myself to be victorious despite all odds, it became an important fuel for my success. Little did I know that all those accomplishments (both recognized and unrecognized) were preparing me to be on a very short list of the "Lucky." Everyone knows this list very well. Many of you have been the receiver of these comments, or the sender:

"They were just lucky."

"They were just in the right place at the right time."

"They didn't do much to get that."

When in fact, I "they/we" did a lot to get to that perfectly timed moment and be the recipients of such fortune. It was through will, determination, and circumstance. Through it all, the actions and steps I took to get there were not premeditated. Meaning, I wasn't expecting that if I did this, I would get that. Luck and timing should not be intentional! I would have several other situations of recognition throughout my career. I would find my solace and victory in receiving a thank you from others who would witness my accomplishments; receiving them prepared me the most for the opportunity presented to me near the end of my military career.

About ten years later, I would face a decision made by my leadership that I found very disappointing then. It turned out to be what a battle buddy of mine calls a "trust the process" decision that I now look back on as the best decision of my military career. It was 2003, and I had been selected for promotion to sergeant major. I would now become a student at the United States Army Sergeants Major Academy (USASMA), commonly referred to as the Sergeants Major Academy. In layman's terms, it's a one-year university for newly selected and promoted E-9s.

At approximately seven months into the course, classmates begin to receive follow-on reassignment orders. If you can imagine three hundred and eighty-eight sergeants major and sergeants major select full of high-level senior leadership knowledge and ready to reengage the force, you know that all of us wanted the highest profile assignment the Army, Reserve, or National Guard had to offer (well, most of us, anyway). As the assignments began flowing in, excited and disappointed conversations took place. There were some who loved their assignments and others who did not, but that's the life of a soldier; you go where the Army needs you. I knew that my career to this point had been one dedicated to the Army and leadership. I knew that I had done what the Army asked of me without question or discernment. I also knew the key assignments the National Guard had to offer and felt confident that I would be placed in one.

I received my orders one month before graduation. I had been ordered to report to the office of the Army National Guard Equal Opportunity and Civil Rights. As important as this office and position is, it wasn't one of the high-visibility positions that an E-9 progresses through for follow-on assignments to high-profile positions in the Guard. I was pissed off because it's a minority position that minorities are assigned to. At the time, I couldn't see through the fact that all my white male sergeant major counterparts were being assigned into the high-visibility positions.

This seriously distracted me from focusing on my new assignment. I was so furious that on my first day in the office and during my first meeting with my new leadership, I told him I had a hidden agenda that wasn't in line with the organization's goals. That agenda was that I was aggressively seeking reassignment into a position that had visibility from upper leadership that eventually could get me to my ultimate assignment of becoming the command sergeant major of the Army National Guard. I wanted the whole thing; I felt that leadership sticking me in a position that none of them truly focused on was a setback to my career. I'll never forget Mr. Felton Page's response:

"The position doesn't make you; you make the position."

He went on to explain what he meant in great detail. I knew what he meant as soon as he said it. My life flashed before me, back to my first assignment in Korea where I made the mental decision to be in this not for me, but for my soldiers. I realized at that moment that I had forgotten my original mission statement.

I've had some great commanders, supervisors, and leaders, and Felton Page is in this special category. We would go on to do many great things for the Equal Opportunity and Civil Rights Program. I couldn't have been prouder to become the Equal Opportunity sergeant major for the Army National Guard program and truly work with an office of the most sincere and focused professionals of that time.

About one year into my assignment, I had a "keeping it real" moment with Sgt. Maj. Frank Lever, the command sergeant major of the Army National Guard at that time. I know the rule that says men should never converse at the urinals, but I saw the shot, and there was no danger, so I took it!

"Sergeant Major, it really pissed me off that I was assigned to the EO SGM position while everyone else went on to more visible positions. Why does the EO Office have to be filled with a minority anyway? Just because I'm black didn't mean I was the only one who could have done this job. I will tell you now that I was, but that still didn't make it right." (Yes, we were still at the urinals. It was a long day).

He looked right at me and said, "Vic, I selected you for that position because I knew you were the right person for that job."

Maybe I should've had that conversation with him a year earlier? I didn't feel that an apology was warranted; what I needed to do was tell him from the bottom of my heart, thank you. Once again, there was another person in my life outside of my family and immediate friends who knew my worth and the value I bring to a team. Command Sgt. Maj. Anthony "Tony T" Traylor was right: you must TRUST THE PROCESS!

The beast represents every challenge you've ever faced or will face. When you step into situations without any preparation, let's face it, you get what you get! Now if you step into that same situation prepared and equipped with everything you need, then you get what you deserve! I call all of those challenges the BEAST, and she comes in many forms. I often referred to the beast of the National Guard as a mad bull that has been throwing riders since 1636. The epitome of leadership is to sit in the saddle on the bull and ride her for eight seconds — or in military years, twenty years of active federal service.

The key is to understand all the regulations, policies, and procedures, as well as adhere to them. You can't just know what they say; you must also do what they say.

We call that "what right looks like." In recent years, we have had some great leaders fall through selfish acts of their own. Many of these leaders have successfully accomplished great things that should be emulated and other things that should not. That's why following the leader can be good and can also be extremely bad, but learning from that leader's successes and failures is exceptional!

I remember sharing my thoughts on how I believed anyone could successfully maneuver through the Guard during one of my training sessions with my soldiers. I was layers deep into a conversation on the "Army Umbrella," using it as the metaphor for true loyalty (not the discussion on should the Army be allowed to carry one, as we all know... It rains on the Army, not in it!). The umbrella I'm referring to represents the big picture of loyalty and where a soldier places his true altruism. Loyalty has just as many levels as the Army does corps, divisions, brigades, battalions, companies, platoons, squads, or sections. Every person who falls under any of those commands are told to be loyal to them. That would often mean going against a higher command or a sister company, creating ethical situations and putting soldiers in an uncomfortable and at times unlawful situation. I was faced with a situation as a young staff sergeant (E-6) where I was asked where my loyalty lay, with the command or somewhere else? I told this captain that my loyalty was to the United States Army, and since this command fell under the Army's umbrella, there was no question that I am loyal to it. That question was asked of me because I was being asked to falsify a document. Let's just say that since I didn't go along, we didn't get along.

I shared that story with my team as an example of the decisions we're often faced with making and how so many times we don't make the right ones for fear of acceptance. I look for confirmation in any message I deliver or speech I give by individual interactions after I'm done. After this session, one of my high-speeds walked up to me with that infectious smile and "always on" motivation he had.

"Sergeant Major, I love that beast speech! It all makes sense to me now. I'm going to take that with me wherever I go."

Kevin, I hope you've tamed all the beasts in your life!

7

Self-evaluation

"Self-knowledge involves relationship. To know oneself is to study oneself in action with another person. Relationship is a process of self-evaluation and self-revelation. Relationship is the mirror in which you discover yourself. To be is to be related."

Bruce Lee

I STARTED SELF-EVALUATING myself when I was seventeen. I distinctly remember that because I was just beginning to have an ounce of self-confidence coinciding with the introduction of girls in my life. I had an epiphany after three girls argued over which of a group of five guys, including me, looked the best.

I don't think any of the other guys saw the conversation the way I did. The qualities the girls were looking for in us really fascinated me. One would yell to the rest of the group, "Oh no, girl, he's the cutest," followed by "I like his muscles," and then I heard, "He has a nice smile." I use the terms "girls" and "boys" because although we were teenagers, I don't believe any of us knew anything about life or could define "quality." Each of them chose a different person as the "cutest," and I had to ask myself why was that? Lucky for me, I made the list. That could have been a serious character killer.

After that, I began self-evaluating myself to work on improving those qualities the girls saw in the rest of the guys. I believe that stemmed from my OCD. The same perfection I strive for in my external life is triple the effort I put into my internal self. The fastest way I know how to get true updates is through evaluating myself. My absolute worst critic of myself is me. That doesn't mean I'm always putting myself down — although I admit to doing that a lot. Still, on many occasions I put myself *up*, when I know I need it. My mom may have been my biggest fan, but I am my number one supporter!

That's why when I want a true assessment of myself, I take it to the *group* — those people closest to me at that particular time. They offer me real feedback, which is very important. I use it to gauge myself against personal performance marks I've set since about the age of twenty. It's my moral compass that "Seen" created all those years ago, and I use the group to tell me what I'm not seeing within myself.

Each of these evaluations answered one question for me: Did I buy in? And if I bought in, how deep was I? Buying in wasn't a bad thing for me as long as it aligned with my personal agenda, which carried my character that protects my soul. I never could see myself buying into something that didn't align with my character, because I knew I would lose my soul, and losing my soul is never an option and definitely nonnegotiable. If you really want to know how you're doing, have the courage to ask the question to people in and out of your networks and be prepared to accept the answer.

It's hard to imagine life without email; I recall a time in the not so distant past where it was so new that policy was created to have soldiers check their professional email accounts twice a day, after first formation and prior to being dismissed at the end of the day. Email became important to me once I reached leaders ranks and was in charge. I would send out monthly emails with a subject line that read: How Am I Doing? And I would request true and honest feedback, tactfully, of course.

My reasoning was that if I was truly doing something wrong as a leader, the only way we could get better was by me knowing. I stressed the "we" because my actions affect the whole, and that's everyone under my command of authority. It's easy to do this when you're in charge of a small group; it gets a lot more time-consuming as your group grows.

I will never forget an email response I received from one of my peers and fellow senior NCOs after I sent out a massive email to everyone within my span of control as the Equal Opportunity sergeant major for the entire Army National Guard, asking once again, "How am I Doing?" He responded, "Vic, you sure you wanna do that? You might get something back you don't want to hear." I think a lot of leaders feel this way and don't ask because internally they're aware that something is broken, and it's more than likely them or something that's very close to them (this is how houses built of straws are created).

I thought that was a classic response and one that I'm very comfortable with facing. I really believe that God puts checkpoints on the road of our lives just to let us know if we are on course or how far off course we have gotten. I got another one of these moments at a checkpoint I had in Dearborn, Michigan, where I attended the Enlisted Association of the National Guard of the United States (EANGUS) as the interim command sergeant major. Being a guest of honor to an annual national event that brings the enlisted force of the National Guard together for a conference is a very big deal. The Michigan National Guard hosted the conference. It was truly an honor to be their special guest.

One evening, a few of the Michigan guardsmen invited me to a night out with the troops, which was something I was really looking forward to. I find it easier to talk to most people in their natural habitat, and let's be honest; the bar is where you will get most truths on just about any and every subject. I've found that when it comes to emotions and the truth, all people need is a relaxed environment, their favorite beverage, and the truth usually sets them free!

One thing I've always found cool about spending quality time with the troops in their comfort zone (also known as hanging out) is that you're seen in a different light. Not one that disrespects your position of authority, but one that gains their trust of you in that authority. They see you not only as their leader, but as a person they can truly talk to as well. This was the case with one soldier sitting a few barstools away from me who was standoffish the entire night. Every time I would look over at him, he would have this disturbing and disgruntled look on his face and never said a word.

Once the conversations with all the other soldiers slowed down and they had enough to drink to go enjoy themselves on the dance floor, I made my way over to the soldier and asked if I could sit next to him. He had a classic response: "It's a free country, Sergeant Major, and you are the CSM." He didn't say any of that with a smile on his face.

I smiled — actually, I chuckled — because I liked this guy and couldn't wait to hear his story. Of course, at the time he had no idea that he would be telling me it, and neither did I. I began the conversation by asking him why he looked so pissed off and why he wasn't partying with his buddies. (In the Army, it's common to refer to your coworker as your battle buddy; this is instilled in all of us early on in our careers). Basically, "What's up with you, soldier?"

I smiled the entire time I spoke to him. As the loud music played, his fellow soldiers popped in and out, asking me if I wanted a drink or why was I still sitting down, etc. He didn't answer any of my questions, so I asked him what was it about me that he didn't like — to me, it was clear that I was the problem. He looked me right in my eyes and asked, "Permission to speak freely?"

I thought, *Oh, shit! This is going to be good! Any soldier who starts out a conversation with "permission to speak freely" has a lot to say.* If you aren't thick-skinned and don't have feathers like a duck, so water can roll right off you, you will probably say no to this request! But I had been preparing for that moment my whole life.

"Of course you have my permission, soldier. I wouldn't have it any other way." I can't quote exactly what he said but to paraphrase it, he told me that when he heard that the CSM of the Army National Guard was coming to hang out with them, he wasn't impressed. In his mind, I was an asshole. If I remember nothing else from his words, I will never forget that he initially thought I was an asshole.

The reason he thought this was because most of the leadership he'd met never really cared about soldiers; it was all a dog and pony show, and then they were gone. He told me that he kept waiting for that look most people give when they act like they're engaged but are just playing the part — basically, he was waiting for me to come out of character. But he said I never did, and that's when he felt maybe I did care about what was going on.

I smiled that entire time, because once again in my life, God put someone in front of me that once again acknowledged me for the value I brought to an organization, group, or person. He confirmed that my passion wasn't only seen but also felt. The last thing I asked him was, "Do you go to church?"

I have no idea why I asked him that. I had been dealing with my own struggles in my own faith and my daily battles of walking in Christ and finding my way. That question sparked something in him that I wasn't prepared for; his eyes filled with water and he asked me why I asked him that question. I didn't have an answer. He told me that since his deployment, he was having a rough time being back home. Before he left, he was heavy into the church and I believe involved in the deacon ministry. Since returning from the war, he wasn't sure about the church. He wasn't even sure about his life and had contemplated suicide. He told me that our conversation really meant everything to him and that he was going to his church that Sunday.

We didn't exchange contact information, and I really wish we had. He was a member of the 107th Engineer Battalion, 1431st Engineer Company (SAPPER), better known as Alpha Company, out of Calumet, Michigan. I will never forget that because he presented me with his SAPPER coin. I don't know how many of these coins are given out, but I suspect very few, and the gesture brought a tear to my eyes.

I was very honored to receive that coin. I have a considerably large coin collection at my home office and it's displayed there as one of my most prized possessions. The motto of the 107th Engineer Battalion is "Good as Done." I hope that soldier is living that motto to this day, has his life in order, is walking with Christ, and he's good as done.

8

The Crossroad

"Luck is what happens when preparation meets opportunity."

Seneca

THERE'S ANOTHER NAME I must mention, and this chapter is dedicated to him. His name is Maj. Gen. (Ret.) Raymond Carpenter. He was the acting director of the Army National Guard after the retirement of Lt. Gen. Clyde Vaughn, who served as the director from 2005 until early 2009. I didn't know much about Carpenter in early 2009. What I did know was that he truly was a soldier's soldier: soldiers were comfortable around him and he had a natural flow that brought out the best in anyone that was around him.

There are two key moments where our paths crossed that will always remain fresh in my mind, as if they happened yesterday. The first occurred during our semi-annual Army Physical Fitness Test (APFT) during the end of the two-mile run, which was the last event of a three-part fitness test: the push-up, sit-up, and run. It's rare to have a general officer testing with the troops and Carpenter was the exception, as he was in great physical shape and to my recollection, always tested with the troops. He and I congratulated the soldiers crossing the finish line and encouraged others who were cutting it close to their maximum finishing times. (A soldier must complete the two-mile run within a maximum time authorized based on their age and gender.) I recall making a comment to him that it's always good to see a general officer — and not just any officer, but the director of the Army National Guard — at your fitness event.

The second was during the Army's annual ten-mile run, The Army Ten-Miler or ATM as we call it. I was running this race for my fifth consecutive year and didn't know that he was no stranger to it either. We spoke on the first mile of the run in passing, as we both were finding our groove and settling into our pace for the next ten miles. Those two natural encounters covered three principles I've talked about here: fitness, tenacity, and preparation.

It hasn't been an easy journey, but it has been worth it. I've sat in the position as a squad leader, and although that was a tough transition from being one of the soldiers to leading soldiers, I made it through, and it was worth the trials and tribulations. I've been the platoon sergeant, or the "Platoon Daddy" as it was often referred to in the past. It may have only been for a small group of brilliant-minded aviators, operators, and aviation mechanics, but like all soldiers good and bad, they kept me engaged. Every senior enlisted leader will tell you that the greatest position to achieve is that of the Company First Sergeant, also addressed as TOP, and commonly referred to as "the Father of the unit." I learned a lot about soldiers from that position. I learned more about leading — mainly that when you are put in charge, be in charge, because people are relying on you or secretly conspiring against you, which is an ongoing chess game as well.

The kid that I brought along with me all those years was extremely happy because of a critical conversation I had when it was announced that I would be promoted to the rank of sergeant major (E-9). At the time, I was the first sergeant of the Operational Support Airlift Agency stationed at Davison Army Airfield located near Fort Belvoir, Virginia. I'd been in that position for approximately two years and had earned the complete trust of the soldiers appointed under me. That was a humbling experience and a very memorable one as well. I was introduced to yet another valuable learning point: good news isn't always good news for everybody. I was in the middle of our weekly enlisted training session that we referred to as "Sergeant's Time" when the battalion CSM walked into my session to announce that I'd been selected for promotion to sergeant major. I had so many emotions going through my head at the time, the first being the road I took to get here and the many challenges I faced along the journey. I was also thinking to myself, *I need to finish this training, so let's not celebrate too soon; we still have 30 minutes remaining.*

During all this celebration and emotional rollercoaster ride, I noticed that a few soldiers had looks of concern on their faces. You know, the one where if you could see the look on your own face, you'd just stop trying to be happy, knowing that you really aren't.

The thought on my mind from looking at their faces was, *did someone just die?* The irony of that thought was that in their mind someone did, and that someone was me. You see, what they instantly knew was that my promotion meant that I would no longer be their first sergeant. How do you smile in victory, when most of your team is saddened? That was confirmation for Sean (my inner child) that I had not lost my way. What was even more insightful was what the soldier said next:

"Every sergeant major I know is an ass-hole. You're going to become one of [them] now." *(Interesting, huh? Remember the conversation I had with the SAPPER in Minnesota?)* That one did make me laugh — a laugh of, "Wow, guys, I'm glad you know me and appreciate me that much, but I assure you, I will not become an asshole, okay." Those seemed to be the winning words as the congratulations and celebrations began.

I left OSAA for my follow-on assignment to the United States Army Sergeants Major Academy at Biggs Army Airfield (AAF) at Fort Bliss, Texas. There I met more than six hundred fifty sergeants major and sergeants major select — far too many to name individually, and all of them being recognized by the greatest class USASMA has ever had, Class 55 (Double Nickel).

I would graduate from the one-year course and begin my assignment as sergeant major of the Army National Guard Equal Opportunity. I worked with some of the best civilians in the Guard and a truly joint team that kept me engaged. Air National Guard Chief Master Sgt. Melvene Lanier left a Fortune 100 company to do her part for the Air Guard mission. Master Sgt. Artri Spratling is a former Tops in Blue performer who managed a large portion of the programs in the department.

Managing the Equal Opportunity program for fifty states, three territories, and the District of Columbia was a very challenging position that required lots of traveling, many phone conversations, and so many emails I still wonder if I answered them all. It was, and in my opinion, remains the National Guard's most visible and highest priority office. That position allowed me to find the true pulse of the National Guard. It's a very visible and personal position that truly engages the force in a face-to-face setting. The states are managed by an awesome group of professions called State Equal Employment Managers (SEEM). They represent their states very well and are the true pulse of each of them. I truly enjoyed working with each of them and creating positive results.

More luck would come my way (remember: the road of preparation intersects at the road of opportunity, which is where luck interchanges) when I would have the opportunity to apply for the position as the command sergeant major of the Operational Support Airlift Command (OSACOM) and would be selected. Up to that point, all I would have needed for my life to be complete was for the Fort Belvoir military post paper to run a headline article that read "Hometown Hero Returns Home."

OSAA was where I started my National Guard career in 1995, after serving seven years' active duty Army before switching over into the Active Guard and Reserve (AGR) program of the National Guard. The aviation world is a small world in any component. It's a pretty good assumption that you'll see a command and people in your field of expertise again at some point in your career. It was good to be back home and working alongside my latest command team, Col. Michael Bishop.

Bishop was truly a forward thinker, and not someone who would win the popular vote in school. (Sorry, sir. Just sayin'.) Let me be clear, that is not an insult, because Bishop recognized that he was the future of the organization; therefore, he worked in the future. He wasn't a leader that would see end-of-the-year funding (remember use it or lose it?) and blow it on new office furniture, flat-screen TVs, vehicles, etc. If we didn't use it, we lost it and clearly didn't need it. Sometimes when you come out of the storm and look back at it, you realize how bad it wasn't, compared to how bad you thought it would be, causing you to hate the experience while not learning from it until it was over.

I've worked alongside some very impressive officers, with Bishop being one of them. His expectation of leaders appointed under him was that you knew your shit; initially I thought his micromanagement was over the top. He was someone who got in the weeds in areas a battalion commander shouldn't be, but I couldn't have been more wrong. I was right about his expectations of the leaders appointed under his command; where I was wrong was why he got into the weeds. The absolute worst thing you could say to Col. Bishop was "How."

"How" was like saying "Sure, come on in" to a vampire. I don't know any vampires, nor have I received any confirmation that they're real, but according to folklore, the only way a vampire can enter your home is you must invite them. Bishop is no vampire; however, the same rules apply here. If you don't want the boss micromanaging your task, don't invite him in by asking that dreaded question: How would you like that completed? How much time do I have? How, how, how? And for the love of God, please don't say: I don't know how!

He stood tall as a defender at the front gates of ensuring leaders led. Remember what I said earlier? When in charge, be in charge. We developed into a very good battle rhythm. We were a great command team, we engaged our troops, and we both allowed each other to lead from the positions assigned, meaning he never questioned my authority in front of or not in front of the troops no matter the rank, and I made it a point to not discredit his decision. We had a very good command which allowed us to take advantage of our favorite sport, running! I would get mine in early by running every morning and most of the time finishing just before the First Sergeant would call "fall in" for the company's physical training (PT) began, and he would get his every day at noon running the airfield also.

One afternoon, while the colonel was out on his airfield run, I received a call from the chief of staff at the Army Readiness Center. It was headquarters for the director of the Army National Guard as well as the functional active National Guard that managed the programs of each National Guard state organization.

"Good afternoon. Operational Support Airlift Command, Command Sergeant Major Angry speaking. How may I help you, sir or ma'am?"

"Hi, Sergeant Major. Colonel Stark here. Is Colonel Bishop in?"

"No, ma'am. He's out on his clockwork airfield run. If you like, I can have him call you when he's back in the office."

"Yes, please. That would be fine."

"I may as well let you know what the call is about, and you can discuss it with him before he calls back. Major General Carpenter would like for you to fill the position as the interim command sergeant major until such time as they find a replacement for John Gipe."

"Ooookay," I said. "Well, I can tell you his answer now. He'll probably say something like, "'When do you start?'" But I'll still speak with him about it, and we will give you a call shortly."

A great command team should have communications so open that if I'm in my office, on the phone, in the middle of a detailed conversation, the other half of my command team can walk into my office and flop down in the chair in front of my desk just to chat, and vice versa with roles reversed. That's a pretty effective command team.

Like clockwork, at 1300, the "old man" (a reference the colonel gets in a military unit — yes, it could be an old woman as well) is back in uniform and sitting at his desk. I walked across the hall and into his command section, greeting Roxy first, as always: "Good afternoon, Roxy. I'm going to be in with the colonel for a few minutes, OK."

I walked in and flopped down in the chair located in front of his desk.

COL Bishop: "What's up CSM?" asked Col. Bishop. "What you got going on for the afternoon?"

"Well, sir, while you were out running, I got a pretty interesting call from Colonel Stark. She relayed a request from General Carpenter that he wanted me to fill in as the CSM of the Guard."

"Well, I hope you told her yes!" from Colonel Bishop.

"I told her you would say that, sir. I also told her that we would call her back as soon as you and I spoke."

That conversation occurred on a Thursday. I had an office call with MG Carpenter the next day to discuss the details of the temporary assignment. It was a really good conversation that ended with me asking, "So, sir, when do I start?"

His response was, "NOW."

I prepared myself for every opportunity, and it resulted in the greatest luck I've had in my military career — but that's another story.

Made in the USA
Lexington, KY
08 October 2018